From Tepees to Towers

A Photographic History of American Architecture

OVERLEAF: *Vassall-Longfellow House, Cambridge, Massachusetts, 1759.* Built by Major John Vassall, this dignified frame, Georgian house served as Washington's headquarters from 1775–1776, and was the home of the poet Henry Wadsworth Longfellow from 1837–1882. A formal facade features four two-story pilasters, a pediment with a fanlight, a dentillated cornice under the eaves, and a balustrade around four sides of the roof.

From Tepees to Towers

A Photographic History of American Architecture

by Carl E. Hiller

LITTLE, BROWN AND COMPANY *Boston Toronto*

Published simultaneously in Canada
by Little, Brown & Company (Canada) Limited

PRINTED IN THE UNITED STATES OF AMERICA

Contents

Acknowledgments

The author wishes to thank Ellen Marsh, Ruth Myers, John Bradford, Milton Brown, Jack Lowery, and James E. Tobin for their advice, help and encouragement in the preparation of this book.

To my parents

Introduction

SHELTER is one of man's basic needs. Throughout history and in every part of the world the nature of human shelter has been governed by several primary factors: the purpose of the building, the prevailing climate, and the materials available. Added to these is an important, though almost indefinable factor: man's urge to adorn, that creative impulse which may cause what he builds to be beautiful as well as functional. Endowed with this aesthetic quality, building becomes architecture.

The purposes for which men build are many. They build to provide shelter for living, for worship, for government, for learning, for business, for amusement. In each case a simple form that served its purpose when life was simple has become complex, as life in our society has become more complex. The one-room schoolhouse has given way to a many-winged educational plant; the single-family dwelling to a multi-unit apartment house. A small general store has become a giant department store; a single-room railroad station has mushroomed into a huge terminal. New forms have been created to serve new functions: many-celled office buildings and sprawling airport terminals.

Climatic conditions also dictate the shape of man's building. The steeply pitched roof of northern climates sheds the snow. Broad, over-hanging eaves in tropical regions provide cool shade. Tall, narrow build-ings are more efficient where heating is needed, whereas low, spreading buildings are fine where central heating is not necessary.

The materials that are available affect the form and appearance of buildings. In heavily forested northern countries wood is used extensively. In southern regions of Europe, as in the southwestern United States, where wood is scarce, brick, stone, and adobe are common building materials.

To trace the development of architecture is to trace the history of man and his civilization. In the United States the development of architecture, from that of the Indians to that of the present day, is a fascinating story that is still in the making.

1 The Indians as Builders

THE NATIVE AMERICANS found by the first European explorers of the New World included diverse groups of people inhabiting many regions of the continent. Called Indians by the explorers, who had expected to reach the Indies by traveling west across the Atlantic, these people lived in the forests of the eastern and western shores, in the southern swamps, on the great central and western plains, and in the southwestern desert country. Each group had developed a distinct culture or way of life, shaped by the climate they lived in, the foods they ate, the need to defend themselves from other groups. Their cultures were relatively simple or primitive ones, in which hunting, fishing, raising crops and domestic animals, and making war, were of chief concern. Their dwellings reflected their ways of life.

Model of an Indian long house. The Iroquois and other tribes of the Northeast — and also the Puget Sound Indians of the Northwest — built similar homes. They were multiple dwellings, sometimes 125 feet long, housing several families. A framework of bent saplings was covered with overlapping rows of bark, in much the way shingles are used today.

1

2

A tepee of the Cheyenne Indians. The Cheyenne roamed the great plains of South Dakota, Colorado, Wyoming, and Montana in search of buffalo and other game. A frame of long poles covered with animal hides — usually buffalo or deer — served as an easily portable home. When the Indians moved to new hunting grounds it was the job of the women to dismantle the tepee and set it up on the new site.

A Navajo hogan, Arizona. The Navajos, principally shepherds, moved occasionally to provide better grazing lands for their flocks. This shelter of earth and logs served as a winter home. In summer, airier structures of branches and grass were used.

3

4

The Pueblo of Taos in northern New Mexico. Built of adobe, a pueblo was both home and fortress for the agricultural Indians of the Southwest. Access to the cubelike rooms was through trapdoors in the roofs, reached by ladders. In time of enemy attack, the ladders were pulled up. This pueblo has been inhabited continuously since about 1700.

2 Colonial America

THE EARLY COLONISTS who settled in the New World brought with them their languages, their customs and ways of living, and their architecture. They continued to build in the new country as they had built in the old — the English all up and down the Eastern seaboard, the Dutch in the Hudson Valley, the Swedes in Delaware, the Germans in Pennsylvania, the French in New York State and Louisiana, and the Spanish in the Southwest. In almost every instance, however, they changed their various styles in some way, according to the climate and to the materials they found in the new country.

The earliest houses of the most numerous of the colonists, the English, were extremely simple. They were rectangular boxes topped with steeply pitched roofs. Construction consisted of a heavy timber frame filled in with brick, stones, or wattle and daub, with an outer, protective layer of shingles or clapboard. The most common plan in the seventeenth century was for two large rooms separated by a chimney whose fireplaces heated both rooms and served for cooking as well. Elaborations on this plan included second-story rooms and additions (ells) in the rear. Small casement windows were typical, with panes of oiled paper, since glass had to be imported from England and was expensive.

Later colonial houses in the eighteenth century usually consisted of four rooms on a floor, opening off a central hall. Chimneys were then placed at the outer (gable) ends of the house. Symmetrical and more formal in appearance than the earlier, more picturesque buildings, these houses began to use window and door ornamentation. The front door became the chief feature of the facade, and was usually topped by a transom light or — a more elaborate form — a fanlight.

5

*Parson Capen House, Topsfield, Massachusetts, built about 1683.
The English colonists of the Northeast imitated the houses
they had known in the Old World. Typical of this earliest
Colonial type are the steep roof, small casement windows,
second-story overhang, and massive central chimney.*

ABOVE: *House in Newcastle, Delaware, built about 1700.*
BELOW: *A farmhouse in the district of Schoonebeek, Holland.*
The Dutch colonists who settled in New York, New Jersey,
and Delaware copied the homes in Holland that they had
left behind, as can be seen in the similarity of these two
houses with their broad, overhanging eaves.

8

ABOVE: *Buildings of the Alte Hofhaltung in Bamberg, Germany.*
BELOW: *The Cloisters at Ephrata, Pennsylvania, built in 1741*
by members of a religious sect who had emigrated from
Germany. The stark wooden buildings, with their steep
roofs and tiny dormer windows, show close relationship to
the German buildings pictured above.

9

ABOVE: *A farmhouse of the Loire Valley region of France.*
BELOW: *The Abraham Hasbrouck House in New Paltz, New York, built about 1712.* New Paltz was founded by French Huguenots who, fleeing religious persecution in France, settled in the Hudson Valley, where they built low, stone homes like those of their native country.

Houses on Bourbon Street, New Orleans, Louisiana. The French who settled in the lower Mississippi Valley built plantation and town houses derived from the architecture of their native land. These houses are typical of the French Quarter of New Orleans, with their second-story balconies and graceful iron work decoration.

Church of San Francisco de Taos, Ranchos de Taos, New Mexico, built about 1772 by Franciscan missionaries who adapted and simplified the Renaissance style of Spain, using adobe — the same material used by the Indians in nearby Taos Pueblo. The thick walls and massive buttresses give it a feeling of great strength and solidity.

ABOVE: *The Mission Church of San José in San Antonio, Texas, begun in 1768 by Spanish missionaries.* The very ornate entrance, derived from the Spanish Baroque style, is in sharp contrast to the plain, unbroken surface of the rest of the facade.

BELOW: *One of a chain of California missions* stretching from San Diego to the San Francisco Bay area, this one at Santa Barbara was built by Franciscan missionaries. Its twin belfries are simplified versions of those found on Spanish churches of the period.

3 Houses from Handbooks

THE LATE RENAISSANCE, or Baroque, flowering in England in the eighteenth century during the reigns of the Hanoverian kings, George I, II, and III, produced a style of architecture we call Georgian. Since the political, economic, and social ties of the colonies were with England, it was natural for them to import its prevailing architectural style. The Georgian style, formal and dignified in character, was well suited to large houses and mansions, to churches, and to civic buildings such as town halls and colonial capitols. In New England wood was a common material, even for details like columns, pilasters, and pediments. In New York and Pennsylvania the native stone was chiefly used, and in the Southern colonies brick was the most widely-used material.

Architects as such were almost nonexistent at the time. Master carpenters, working from handbooks for the most part imported from England, executed some of the best examples of Georgian architecture. In many instances the builders introduced variations and embellishments of their own. Added to these the regional differences resulted in a richly varied American Georgian style.

16

The Wentworth-Gardner House in Portsmouth, New Hampshire, 1760. One of the best examples of early Georgian houses. Its facade, including the white quoins at the corners, is of wood, imitating stone, and is dominated by a handsome doorway with a four-light transom and a broken-scroll pediment.

A Georgian house in Litchfield, Connecticut, built by Elisha Sheldon in 1760. About 1800 a local builder, William Spratt, added the columned entrance with the Palladian window and pediment above it, as well as the cornices over the first-story windows and under the eaves.

18   *Interior of Congregation Jeshuat Israel (called the Touro Synagogue), Newport, Rhode Island, 1763.* Built by Peter Harrison, who took the idea from a handbook of the designs of the English architect, Inigo Jones, it is considered one of the most beautiful early church interiors.

19   *Mount Pleasant, Philadelphia, Pennsylvania, 1761–1762*. A good example of a formal manor house of the Middle Atlantic states, it has a facade of buff stucco, set off by white window and door trim. As was also the custom in many Southern mansions, the kitchen and servants' quarters were housed in the out-buildings at either side of the main house.

The Capitol, Williamsburg, Virginia, 1751–1753, restored 1928–1934. It was in the original red-brick, symmetrical Georgian building, when Williamsburg was the capital of Virginia, that Patrick Henry gave the speech that made him famous.   20

Residence of Miles Brewton, Charleston, South Carolina, 1769. 21
A dignified Georgian town house of the South, it boasts a
two-story portico, with pediment and dentillated cornices.

*Westover, residence of William Byrd II, Charles City County,
Virginia, built about 1730.* A Georgian plantation house, with
a steep, hipped roof, dormer windows, tall, twin chimneys
at each end of the main building. The large central doorway
is topped by a curved pediment. 22

4 Buildings for a New Nation

THE NEW NATION was born. Having achieved political independence, the thirteen colonies hugging the eastern seaboard of North America drafted a constitution establishing a Federal government and separate state governments. Buildings to house the governmental bodies were needed, as were buildings for schools, universities, and libraries.

To design these buildings the new Republic depended on architects trained in Europe, or on men with no formal, professional training in architecture. Thomas Jefferson, the third President of the new country, was such an amateur, a man of many interests. As Ambassador to France, before he became president, he had traveled widely in that country, and had been particularly impressed by the Roman ruins in southern France. He sensed a relationship between the Roman Republic and the new American nation and he felt that the architecture of Rome would be a fitting style for the public buildings of the United States. His design for the state capitol of Virginia at Richmond was inspired by one of the Roman temples he had seen in France, the Maison Carrée at Nîmes.

Jefferson's most important design, perhaps, was that for the University of Virginia at Charlottesville. His plan for the campus included a mall dominated at one end by a domed library and flanked by a series of small, temple-like buildings connected by a colonnade. The design was masterful in its dignity, cohesiveness, and functionalism. It is to this day a model for college campuses.

In designing his own house, Monticello, Jefferson used as his model an adaptation of a Roman building by the Italian Renaissance architect, Palladio. Monticello is a handsome, red-brick building, topped by a low dome, and ornamented with a portico and white columns.

The architects trained abroad were responsible for some of the most important buildings of the new Republic. One of them was William Thornton, who drew up the first plans for the Capitol in Washington. Another was James Hoban, a young Irishman who designed the White House in 1792, and also worked on designs for the Capitol.

But the Capitol as we know it today was largely the work of Benjamin Latrobe, who had received his training in Germany and England. He produced the designs for it, and supervised both the original construction and its reconstruction after the British burned it during the War of 1812.

A native of Salem, Massachusetts, Samuel McIntire was trained as a master carpenter and woodcarver. Full of imagination and great creative ability, he studied books on architecture, particularly those by Robert and James Adam of Scotland. The brothers Adam, inspired by engravings of Roman ruins, had adapted many of the classical details and motifs as interior and exterior ornamentation on buildings.

Salem at the time was one of the most prosperous cities on the Atlantic coast, the seaport from which the first ships went out to trade with China and the Far East. Its merchants and sea captains became wealthy in the China trade, and it was for them that McIntire designed his finest mansions. They are known for their handsome and dignified three-story facades and for the delicately beautiful carvings on their interior walls, ceilings, doorways, and fireplaces.

Charles Bulfinch, another native New Englander, was educated at Harvard and practiced the profession of architecture in Boston. Also influenced by the Adam brothers and the Georgian architecture of England, he designed many of Boston's admired churches, homes, and public buildings, including New North Church, New South Church, Faneuil Hall, and the State House. He also designed the Connecticut State House in Hartford and buildings for Harvard and for Phillips Academy at Andover.

A man who was indirectly responsible for many good examples of Federal architecture was Asher Benjamin of Greenfield, Massachusetts. Benjamin wrote the first original book on architecture to be printed in America, *The Country Builder's Assistant*, as well as six other architectural handbooks. These books were used by carpenters all over the country who, although they might change and adapt Benjamin's designs, reproduced his basic ideas.

Monticello, home of Thomas Jefferson, Charlottesville, Virginia, 1770–1809. Jefferson himself designed the house, modeling it after the mansion in Vicenza, Italy (BELOW), designed by the Italian architect Palladio, called the Villa Rotunda.

24

25

ABOVE: *A Roman temple at Nimes, in the south of France.* Called the Maison Carrée, it was the inspiration for Thomas Jefferson's State Capitol in Richmond, Virginia, 1785–1792, pictured BELOW. The large central section was designed by Jefferson; the other wings were added later.

26

27

The University of Virginia, Charlottesville, Virginia, 1821–1826. Designed by Thomas Jefferson, this was the first state university in the country. Surrounding an open "square" are small classroom buildings connected by roofed colonnades. The large domed building is the library which was destroyed by fire in 1894, and reconstructed. Jefferson's plan for what he called an "academical village" has served as a model for many college and university campuses.

Peirce-Nichols House, Salem, Massachusetts, 1782. Designed by Samuel McIntire, this three-story house is typical of many he built for wealthy shipowners and merchants of Salem. Although entirely of wood, elegance was achieved by the pilasters at the corners, the cornices over the windows, the portico over the main entrance, and the balustrade surmounting the whole.

29

First Congregational Church, Bennington, Vermont, 1806. A carpenter, Lavius Filmore, based his design for this handsome church on a drawing from Asher Benjamin.

The State House, Boston, 1795–1798. Charles Bulfinch designed this dignified capitol for the Commonwealth of Massachusetts. Of red brick, with white trim, it is topped by a gold-leafed dome and a lantern.

Gore Place, Waltham, Massachusetts, 1797–1804. The country house for Governor Gore, this dignified brick mansion has an elliptical living room.

5 The New World Borrows from the Old

BEGINNING about 1820 a succession of Old World architectural styles swept the United States, which was still importing its chief artistic influences from abroad. The first, and possibly the most far-reaching, of the revivals was the Greek.

For several reasons architects and builders naturally looked to the temples of ancient Greece for inspiration. For one thing a middle class was rising in the States, a group which turned to democratic ideals as they had been practiced in the Greek city states of the fifth century B.C. Also, in 1820 the Greek people were in the throes of a struggle for independence from their oppressors, the Turks. Their valiant fight inspired the sympathy of the Western World, especially of the Americans who had so recently been involved in a similar struggle.

One of the leading proponents of the Greek Revival was Benjamin Latrobe, who had been chiefly responsible for the Capitol. Another was Robert Mills, the first man to be trained as an architect in this country. He was an apprentice draftsman for Jefferson at Monticello, and later worked under Latrobe for five years. Although he designed many fine houses and churches, he is probably best known for his two Washington monuments, one in Baltimore and the other in the nation's capital.

The Gothic Revival that followed the Greek was the result of two factors. The romantic trend in all the arts in England during the middle of the nineteenth century caught the imagination of literary and artistic men in the United States. Further, people were tiring of the repetition of Greek temples. Two men who were perhaps most responsible for popularizing the Gothic Revival in this country were Andrew Jackson Downing and Alexander Jackson Davis.

Downing was a writer and critic, the first American to make a profession of landscape design. He was responsible for the idea of naturally landscaped parks in this country. Davis was a disciple of his who designed many Gothic "cottages" as well as houses in other styles like Tudor, Swiss chalet, Egyptian, and Italian. By departing from the formal classical buildings, architects gained a freedom of expression and an ability to suit a building to its site. Most important, they could arrange the rooms of a house with more thought to its function as a place to live in.

Richard Upjohn and James Renwick, Jr. were two important architects of the Gothic Revival. Upjohn, of English birth, created a number of large homes for wealthy New Yorkers and New Englanders and also the present State Capitol of Connecticut at Hartford. He is best known for his design for Trinity Church, at the foot of Wall Street in New York. It stands there now, a dignified structure derived from the English Gothic style, dwarfed by modern skyscrapers.

Renwick, a contemporary of Upjohn, designed many churches, the best known being Grace Church and St. Patrick's Cathedral, both in New York City. The old Smithsonian Institution in Washington, D.C., one of his greatest designs, is a rambling, picturesque structure done in the Romanesque manner.

The Romanesque Revival was another popular style of the mid-1800's. There is hardly a town in the East or Middle West that does not have a bank, railroad station, library, or jail with the squat, almost grim, character of the Romanesque or early Medieval architecture, with its heavy stone or brick, small windows, broad-arched entrances, and turrets.

Even the architecture of ancient Egypt inspired a revival — a short-lived one. It was not easily adaptable to the needs of American builders, nor was it very popular.

ABOVE: *The Parthenon, a Greek temple built in the fifth century* B.C. It was the chief inspiration for thousands of Greek revival buildings in the United States. One of these, seen BELOW, is the Second Bank of the United States, Philadelphia, Pennsylvania, 1818–1824, designed by William Strickland.

33

Girard College, Philadelphia, Pennsylvania, 1833. Thomas U.
Walter was the architect for this Greek revival building. It
is closer than most such buildings to the original Greek
temple form, being surrounded on all four sides by columns.

LEFT: *The Choragic Monument of Lysikrates, Athens, third century* B.C., which became the model for decorative lanterns on such Greek revival buildings as the Merchants' Exchange (BELOW) in Philadelphia, Pennsylvania, built in 1832–1834 by William Strickland.

36

Congregational Church, Litchfield, Connecticut, 1829. A Greek revival church of great grace and dignity surrounded by the tall elms typical of many New England towns. Tall, slender columns front a portico topped by a simple pediment that repeats the lines of the roof.

37

38
Oak Alley, Vacherie, Louisiana, built about 1836. A fine example of a Greek revival Southern plantation house, with great porches running the length of the main and second floors, fronted by a two-story colonnade.

Chambliss House, Nantucket, Massachusetts, 1845–1847. An imposing Greek revival house with modified Corinthian capitals. Nantucket, an island 30 miles off the coast, was an important whaling port. The turret served as a lookout for residents to watch for the returning ships of their menfolk.

39

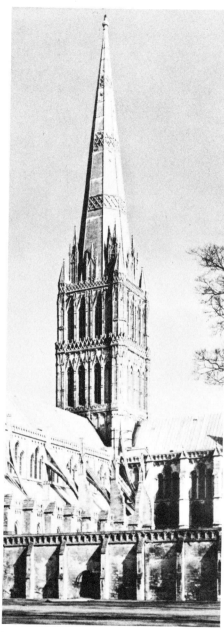

LEFT: *Trinity Church, New York City, 1846.* One of the best examples of Gothic revival architecture, this church was designed by Richard Upjohn. It stands today, dwarfed by the skyscrapers of lower Broadway which surround it. Its kinship to the thirteenth-century English Gothic Salisbury Cathedral (ABOVE) is easily seen.

House of Henry Delamater, Rhinebeck, New York, 1844. A Gothic cottage designed by Alexander Jackson Davis. The decorative scrollwork of wood imitates the stone tracery of European Gothic buildings.

House in Kennebunk, Maine, known as the "Wedding Cake" House. The original Georgian house of brick was built about 1800, and the Gothic wood tracery added about 1850.

BELOW: *Wilson Hall, Dartmouth College Museum, Hanover, New Hampshire, 1884.* One of the many Old World revival styles was the Romanesque, with its heavy masonry, broad, round arches, small windows, and conical towers. Many of these features were inspired by such structures of the Middle Ages as those at Carcassonne (RIGHT), a French walled city built in the thirteenth century.

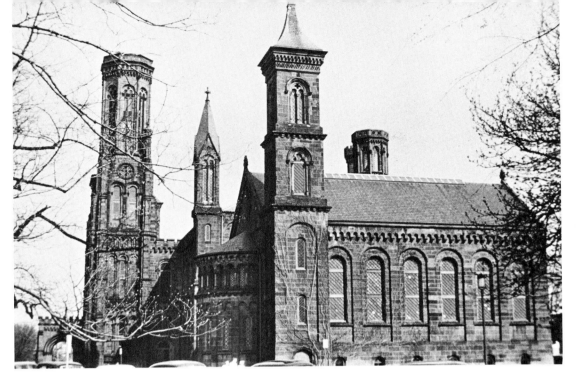

The Smithsonian Institution, Washington, D.C., 1846–1855.
This museum, a rambling collection of buildings, turrets
and towers, was one of the finest achievements of James
Renwick, Jr.

Railroad Station, Hartford, Connecticut. The Romanesque
style was popular also for such public buildings as banks,
libraries, and courthouses.

48

ABOVE: *Grove Street Cemetery, New Haven, Connecticut, 1845–1846*. This gate, designed by Henry Austin, was inspired by the architecture of ancient Egypt. Similar columns, with their lotus bud capitals, can be seen in the Temple of Luxor in Egypt (BELOW).

49

Whalers' Church, Sag Harbor, New York, 1844. Minard Lafever, carpenter and architect, translated the massive character of an Egyptian stone temple into wood for this Long Island Church.

6 Victorian America

DURING and immediately following the Civil War architects and builders erected buildings that could not be classified as belonging to any one historical period or style. Houses, hotels, hospitals, and public buildings were designed with a freedom that seemed to have no formal rules. The mansard roof from France was topped by wrought iron tracery, balconies were edged with ornate wood or cast iron railings, gables and eaves were hung with gingerbread produced by the newly invented scroll saw. Cupolas, towers, and turrets crowned roofs, while rambling porches surrounded the whole. Much of the building of this period has since been criticized as over ornate and even ugly, but it certainly showed vigor and imagination. Historically its freedom of plan and detail paved the way for later architects like Richardson, Sullivan, and Wright, who created order from its chaos.

House in Madison, Wisconsin, about 1860. This Victorian building, with some of the same Italianate features of the one opposite, has a symmetrical facade and a mansard roof capped by ornate iron work.

Victoria Mansion, Portland, Maine, 1859. Henry Austin was the architect for this house in one of the most popular early Victorian styles, the Italianate. Typical features of such houses are the square tower, rounded windows, and overhanging eaves.

House in San Francisco, California, about 1880. One of the
most popular styles of the late Victorian period was called
"Queen Anne." This example is typical of hundreds that
survived the San Francisco earthquake and fire of 1906.
Porches, balconies, turrets, and windows of varied shapes
were all used freely in creating houses for country, suburban,
and city dwellers.

7 Henry Hobson Richardson

EDUCATED AT HARVARD and at the École des Beaux Arts in Paris, Henry Hobson Richardson became the most important architect of his time, and exerted the greatest influence on those who followed him. His reputation was made by work on his first sizable commission, Boston's Trinity Church. For that building, as for much of his later work, he borrowed heavily from the Romanesque style of southern France and Spain. His buildings are usually described therefore as Richardsonian Romanesque.

Richardson's style is characterized by solid heavy masonry, broad round arches, and well-organized grouping of windows. In this style he created numerous libraries, jails, and railroad stations.

Crane Memorial Library, Quincy, Massachusetts, 1880–1883.
This library for a Boston suburb is typical of many of Richardson's public buildings, in its use of stone masonry, broad-arched entrance, and window arrangement.   *54*

45

Trinity Church, Boston, Massachusetts, 1872–1877. Romanesque in inspiration, as were many of Richardson's designs, Trinity Church is probably his most important work.

56

Residence of W. Watts Sherman, Newport, Rhode Island, 1874–1876. This large mansion, built for a wealthy banker, is considered to be one of Richardson's best house designs. Its exterior materials include stone, half-timber, and shingles.

8 McKim, Mead and White

SOME of the finest building in America, from the late nineteenth century to the present, has resulted from the teamwork of two or more architects working together as a firm. Such a partnership was that of McKim, Mead and White, formed in 1879. All three men had gone to Europe for their architectural training. Two of them, Charles F. McKim and Stanford White, had then served their apprenticeship in Richardson's office while he was working on Boston's Trinity Church.

The early work of the firm consisted chiefly of large rambling country homes for wealthy Easterners. Informal in character, and surrounded by broad verandas, these houses were of frame construction covered with shingles left to weather a silvery gray. In their later buildings McKim, Mead and White turned to the architecture of Rome and the French and Italian Renaissance for their inspiration. One of their best-known works was New York's Pennsylvania Station, with its great interior spaces modeled after Rome's Baths of Caracalla. Another was the campus of Columbia University, dominated by the dignified, domed Low Library. For the Boston Public Library, which stands directly across Copley Square from Richardson's Trinity Church, they called in the sculptor St. Gaudens, and the painters, Abbey, Sargent and Puvis de Chavannes, to cooperate in its decoration.

The plans for the World's Columbian Exposition which opened in Chicago in 1893 were largely the work of McKim, Mead and White. They and their colleagues erected a grandiose "White City" on the shores of Lake Michigan, using classical forms. White plaster buildings linked by formal colonnades were reflected in vast lagoons. Thousands of Americans, converging on Chicago from all corners of the country, carried home with them impressions of classic grandeur and dignity. McKim, Mead and White and their fellow architects had thus started a national trend.

ABOVE: *Public Library, Boston, Massachusetts, 1887.* Charles
F. McKim, who was chiefly responsible for this dignified
formal building, took his inspiration from Italian and
French Renaissance designs.

57

BELOW: *Residence of Isaac Bell, Jr., Newport, Rhode Island,
1883.* McKim, Mead and White designed many such rambling and shingled country houses in the Northeast.

58

The Breakers, Newport, Rhode Island, 1892–1895. Richard Morris Hunt designed this "summer cottage" for the railroad magnate, Cornelius Vanderbilt II. Its size and elegance are typical of many such homes that newly-rich industrial barons built during the last part of the nineteenth century. Hunt designed many large, ostentatious homes for both city and country.

59

9 Louis Henri Sullivan

ONE of the architectural giants of America, Sullivan was also a philosopher, deeply impressed by the beauty in nature, and highly poetic in his concepts of architecture. His belief that "form ever follows function" has been a credo of successive generations of architects. He meant that the purpose for which a building is designed indicates what shape it should take. This idea was in direct contrast to that of the classicists of the period, who were letting interior arrangements of their buildings be governed by their classic exteriors.

Louis Henri Sullivan was an Easterner, trained as Richardson had been at the École des Beaux Arts in Paris. Coming to Chicago as a young man, he entered the architectural office of Dankmar Adler and soon became Adler's partner. Adler and Sullivan's chief early commission was the Auditorium Building, combining a hotel, business offices, and a large theatre — a veritable civic center.

Tackling the problems of the steel frame office building, Sullivan produced two fine solutions: the Wainwright Building in St. Louis, and the Guaranty Building (now the Prudential) in Buffalo. He was not content with merely functional construction. He dramatized the vertical character of the buildings by the use of unbroken vertical piers. And to relieve the monotony of regularly spaced windows, he covered the surfaces with fireproof terra cotta tiles in flowing designs derived from nature. Similar designs in terra cotta or cast metal were to become one of his trademarks.

The Chicago building Sullivan created for the Schlesinger and Mayer Company, now the Carson, Pirie, Scott Department Store, was a masterpiece of store architecture. And at the 1893 World's Columbian Exposition, his Transportation Building struck a note of originality in a Fair dominated by traditional classical forms.

52

The Guaranty Building (now the Prudential), Buffalo, New York, 1895, by Adler and Sullivan. The vertical character of this early skyscraper is emphasized by the piers rising between the windows. The severity of the tall building with such regularly spaced windows is relieved by the use of red and green terra cotta decoration between windows and by the ornate cornice.

61

ABOVE: *Detail of the cast iron ornament that decorates the first two stories of the Carson, Pirie, Scott Department Store in Chicago.* In the store (BELOW), originally built for the Schlesinger and Mayer Company in 1899–1904, Sullivan synthesized the horizontal and vertical character in the exterior design, and provided uncluttered display and sales space in the interior.

62

63   *National Farmers' Bank, Owatonna, Minnesota, 1907–1908.*
The first — and best — of a series of small bank buildings
that Sullivan designed for Midwestern towns. It was a
daringly new concept in bank design, providing at once
beauty and the dignity and solidity symbolic of its use.

10 Frank Lloyd Wright

SULLIVAN'S most earnest and talented disciple, Frank Lloyd Wright, is the acclaimed genius of American architecture. His work spanned more than half a century; his tremendous creative power and energy freed architecture from its previous limitations. Setting no single style nor letting successes become patterns, he strove constantly to find fresh approaches to problems.

Wisconsin born, Wright studied engineering at the University of Wisconsin. For six years he worked as a draftsman in the office of Adler and Sullivan, then opened his own office. His early works were chiefly homes in the Chicago suburbs, so-called "Prairie Houses." They are characterized by horizontal masses, broad, overhanging eaves, and gently sloping roofs, reflecting the wide expanse of the Midwestern prairie. In these houses, as in later works, Wright practiced his principle of "organic architecture," "designing from within outward." He planned interiors as "spaces for living," providing areas that flowed into one another instead of the traditional box-like rooms.

His own home, Taliesin ("Shining Brow" in Welsh), hugged a wooded hill near Spring Green, Wisconsin. It exemplifies perfectly his concept that "a building should grow easily from its site." To Taliesin flocked students from all parts of the world to study and work with "the Master." Although Wright died in 1959, the studio and workshop, called the Taliesin Fellowship, goes on.

Wright was for years better known and more admired abroad than in his own country. In 1916 he was commissioned to design a new building for the Imperial Hotel in Tokyo. Tokyo was in an earthquake belt. The problem presented by that fact needed new solutions. Wright, always imaginative and courageous, experimented by using thousands of concrete piers literally to float the building on Tokyo's mud base. He also used cantilevered construction with steel, and a light, native lava rock. His experiments proved successful when, hardly more than a year after the hotel's completion, Tokyo experienced one of the worst earthquakes in its history. The Imperial Hotel was the only large structure in the city to withstand it.

Commissioned by the Johnson Wax Company of Racine, Wisconsin, to design its Administration Building, Wright again experimented, using mushroom-shaped columns to support the roof. Since the columns were narrow at the base, they permitted a maximum use of floor space.

Among Wright's best buildings are his house over a waterfall at Bear Run, Pennsylvania; a store for the V. C. Morris Company in downtown San Francisco; his early Unity Temple in Oak Park, Illinois; and the last work for which he supervised the construction, New York's Guggenheim Museum. For the last he used an entirely new concept of museum design, basing the plan on the idea of a spiral ramp instead of a series of rooms. Visitors to the Museum can take an elevator to the top, then walk leisurely and easily down, viewing the art displays on the way.

Many of the features found in the modern home came from the creative genius of Frank Lloyd Wright. They include indirect lighting, picture windows, and floor heating.

64

Frederick C. Robie House, Chicago, Illinois, 1909. One of the earliest and best of Wright's Prairie Houses, with its long, low, horizontal feeling, and broad overhanging eaves reflecting the open character of the Midwest prairies. Wright also designed the furniture for the house as was often his practice.

ABOVE: *Interior of the living room at Wright's own home, Talie-sin, at Spring Green, Wisconsin.* Some of Wright's "trade-marks" can be seen here: spaciousness, contrasting wood and stone, the large fireplace and hearth, and built-in furniture.

BELOW: *Exterior view of Taliesin, 1925–1959.* The sprawling group of buildings includes studios and workshops for the Taliesin Fellowship, Wright's school. The low stone and stucco buildings, with their broad, overhanging roofs, hug the wooded Wisconsin hilltop of which they seem to be a part.

ABOVE: *Interior of Administration Building for Johnson Wax Company, 1939.* A novel and daring solution to the problem of providing air, space, and light in an office building. The columns are 9 inches in diameter at the base; $18\frac{1}{2}$ feet at the top. The ceiling is of glass tubing.

67

BELOW: *Research Tower, S. C. Johnson & Son, Racine, Wisconsin, 1951.* Annexed to the Administration Building, the tower's floors are supported by a reinforced concrete core. A "curtain" of brick and glass tubing forms the walls.

68

Taliesin West, Phoenix, Arizona, 1938–1959. Wright's winter home fits naturally into its rugged desert setting. Great redwood girders, whose angles repeat those of the nearby mountains, support a roof of white canvas through which light is filtered into the interior. Walls are of "desert concrete," a mixture of cement and large native rocks poured into wooden forms.

70   *"Falling Water," residence of E. J. Kaufmann, Bear Run, Pennsylvania, 1936.* This house, one of Wright's masterpieces, takes fullest advantage of its natural setting. Its use of native stone and cantilevered terraces of reinforced concrete make it seem to grow right out of the rocky landscape.

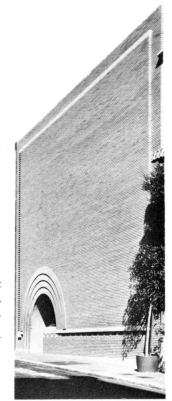

RIGHT: *V. C. Morris Store, San Francisco, California*. For a gift shop in downtown San Francisco, Wright designed an elegant, windowless facade of orange-colored brick, its only opening a tunnel-like entrance. The interior features a spiral ramp leading to the upper floors.

BELOW: *A detail of the entrance.*

73 ABOVE: *Interior of the Guggenheim Museum, New York City, 1959,* featuring a huge spiral ramp for the display of works of art.

BELOW: *Exterior of the Museum,* a bold and novel approach to museum design, this was the last work of Wright's for which he supervised the construction. It is of reinforced concrete, painted a buff color.

74

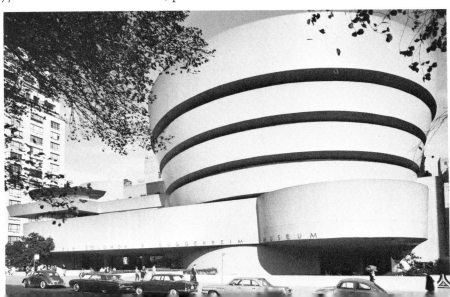

75

ABOVE: *Palace of Fine Arts, San Francisco, California, 1915*. A sentimentally inspired classical building and colonnades of peach-colored stucco designed by Bernard Maybeck for the Panama-Pacific Exposition.

BELOW: *First Church of Christ Scientist, Berkeley, California, 1912*. Maybeck, who founded the School of Architecture at the University of California, showed his great creativity in inventing a new solution for a church building.

76

77

ABOVE: *Residence of D. B. Gamble, Pasadena, California, 1909.*
The brothers Charles S. and Henry M. Greene showed in
their many California houses that the common bungalow
could be beautiful. Their imaginative use of wood, as in this
comfortable-looking house, was one of their strengths.

BELOW: *Residence of Clarence Wyle, Ojai, California, 1948.*
The architect of this airy-looking house is Harwell Hamilton
Harris, a Californian who has been strongly influenced by
the work of Wright and the Greene brothers. In designing
this house — and others — he has brought a highly personal
approach to filling the needs and wishes of his clients.

78

11 Skyscrapers

Two nineteenth-century developments paved the way for the rise of that unique American architectural phenomenon, the skyscraper. One was the perfection of the Bessemer steel process, making available high quality steel beams for construction purposes. The other was the invention of the passenger elevator. The first man to seize the opportunity to use both developments was William Le Baron Jenney, in Chicago. Jenney, trained as an engineer rather than as an architect, invented the steel skeleton, or steel cage, as it is sometimes called. With steel beams for support, exterior walls no longer had to be made to carry the weight of many floors. Greater height was now possible. Jenney's contribution was more practical than aesthetic, enabling others to develop the great business buildings for which Chicago is famous.

Most active in this development were the two architectural firms of Holabird and Roche, and Burnham and Root. William Holabird had gained some of his knowledge of engineering in Jenney's office. In 1886 he and his partner Martin Roche designed the Tacoma Building, since demolished, which was the first structure to use a riveted steel frame. The Chicago "Loop" is still full of the office and store buildings of Holabird and Roche.

Daniel H. Burnham, of the firm of Burnham and Root, first conceived of the idea of the large architect's office, with its various responsibilities delegated to designers, engineers and draftsmen. Burnham, with his partner, John W. Root, was responsible for the design of the sixteen-story Monadnock Building, which was outstanding in its simple, vertical lines, almost to the point of bareness. In their Reliance Building, completed in 1895, they used a type of window which has since become known as the "Chicago window" — a large, horizontal pane, flanked on either side by narrow, movable sashes.

Reliance Building, Chicago, Illinois, 1894–1895. D. H. Burnham and Company were responsible for this skyscraper, one of the earliest to use the steel cage. The combination of broad glass areas ("Chicago windows"), slender vertical piers, and narrow bands of terra cotta ornament express its steel skeleton and give it a light, airy quality.

LEFT: *Woolworth Building, New York City, 1911–1913.* Cass Gilbert, the architect for this 767-foot structure, achieved a soaring feeling by mounting a 25-story tower on a 30-story base, by accenting the vertical lines, and by using Gothic tracery borrowed from Old World cathedrals.

BELOW: *Philadelphia Savings Fund Society Building, Philadelphia, Pennsylvania, 1929–1932.* The architects George Howe and William Lescaze collaborated on the design of this skyscraper, one of the first to utilize the concepts of purity and functionalism of the International Style. Continuous bands of windows permit maximum daylight.

New York Daily News Building, New York City, 1930. In contrast to other buildings of the period, still bearing the stamp of past styles, this structure by Howells and Hood is notable for its simplicity of design. Its vertical emphasis is achieved by white brick walls alternated with unbroken bands of windows and dark spandrels.

82

83

Rockefeller Center, New York City, 1931–1960. A complex of 17 buildings — housing offices, shops, theatres and restaurants — this was the first group of skyscrapers and other buildings planned as a unit. It was the combined work of the firms of Reinhard and Hofmeister, Corbett, Harrison and MacMurray, Hood and Fouilhoux. Its tallest structure, the 70-story RCA Building, towers above 15 acres of buildings and plazas.

84

Lever House, New York City, 1952. An early example of the use of the glass curtain wall, this handsome building is the work of the firm of Skidmore, Owings and Merrill, with Gordon Bunshaft as designer-in-charge. The 24-story tower, sheathed in a blue-green, heat-resistant glass, is balanced by a low, horizontal mass. Most of the ground level is an open area of walks and garden.

United Nations, New York City, 1950. The tall, clean shaft of the Secretariat Building dominates a well-coordinated group of buildings and open spaces overlooking New York's East River. Wallace K. Harrison and Associates, architects for the structure, were influenced by the ideas of Le Corbusier, a member of the board of design.

CBS Building, New York City, 1964. Designed by Eero Saarinen, this 38-story office building was his only skyscraper. Triangular columns sheathed in dark gray granite contain ducts for all mechanical services (electric and telephone cables, heat). A bold, simple shaft, it is the first reinforced concrete office building to be built in New York City.

12 The Twentieth Century: Buildings for a New Era

ARCHITECTURE has probably contributed more than any other art in the twentieth century. The availability and use of new materials, the dependence on engineering and technological innovations, and the employment of the abilities of many people in its realization make it a truly modern art form.

The three great innovators, Richardson, Sullivan, and Wright, paved the way for new generations of architects. Tradition, although not completely tossed aside, has played little part in good contemporary architecture. But new traditions replace old ones, and a twentieth-century architectural style has already become a traditional one.

Called the International Style, it reflects one of the two main streams of thought governing most of contemporary architecture. The International Style, originating at the Bauhaus in Germany, influenced much of Europe's architecture in the 1920's. It was transported to the United States chiefly by two of the Bauhaus architects, Mies van der Rohe and Walter Gropius, both of whom have influenced its spread in this country. Their ideas stress machine technology, geometric cleanness of form and materials. Buildings in this new tradition are impersonal and sometimes cold in feeling.

The other stream in contemporary architecture has no name. Frank Lloyd Wright could be called its father, with his fresh approach to each new problem, use of native materials, and suiting of a building to its site. Structures in this vein tend to be warmer and more personal in feeling, less formal, and to stress the textural qualities of materials. Experimentation with new forms and new materials is more prevalent today than ever, with some of the younger architects taking the lead. The vigor and imagination of these men foretell an exciting future for American architecture.

Offices of Schuckl and Company, Sunnyvale, California, 1942. William W. Wurster, who planned this Administrative Building for a canning company, heads the School of Architecture at the University of California. He is also a member of the firm of Wurster, Bernardi and Emmons, a prolific and popular California firm, whose use of wood textures in houses is notable.

ABOVE: *Northwestern Insurance Company, Los Angeles, California, 1950, by Richard J. Neutra, one of the most influential architects on the West Coast.* In this office building, he used commercially for the first time an ingenious method for controlling the amount of daylight admitted — a series of sunshading, vertical louvers in automatic motion to compensate for the rotation of the earth.

88

BELOW: *House for Mr. & Mrs. Edgar Kaufman, Colorado Desert, 1947.* The elegant, impersonal quality of Neutra's architecture is evident in this desert house, in which interior and exterior seem to flow together.

89

90

Abele House, Framingham, Massachusetts, 1943. Walter Gropius, founder of the Bauhaus in Germany, put into practice some of its principles in designing this house. He approached the problem scientifically — making the best use of the view, placing living room windows so as to take advantage of prevailing breezes for summer cooling, locating the conservatory (at left) to catch the sun, and allowing for future expansion of the second story.

Harvard Graduate Center, Cambridge, Massachusetts, 1950.
Gropius, heading a group called The Architects Collaborative, designed a complex of eight buildings to house Harvard's graduate students. Dominated by a Common Building containing dining halls, lounges and meeting rooms, the group of clean-looking, low buildings are built around large and small quadrangles, which seem like outdoor living rooms.

Geller House, Lawrence, New York, 1945, designed by Marcel Breuer. Breuer, an early disciple of Walter Gropius at the Bauhaus, is well-known for his furniture design as well as his architecture. The simple, interlocking forms of this house result from a synthesis of the purism of the International Style and Breuer's personal creativity.

92

*Apartment buildings at 860 Lake Shore Drive, Chicago, Illinois,
1951.* These steel and glass cubes on stilts overlooking Lake
Michigan were designed by Ludwig Mies van der Rohe,
the architect most influential in the spread of the International Style in the United States.

93

Crown Hall, Illinois Institute of Technology, Chicago, Illinois,
1956. Mies van der Rohe designed this glass-walled building
to house the Institute's Department of Architecture of which
he is Director. Four exterior girders support the roof, elimi-
nating the need for interior columns, thus providing uncluttered floor space. 94

ABOVE: *McGregor Memorial Community Conference Center, Wayne State University, Detroit, Michigan, 1958.* The architect for this beautiful, airy structure was Minoru Yamasaki, a native of Seattle. Set on a platform to give it importance, it achieves richness through its materials: floors and columns of white marble, partitions of plaster and teakwood, and walls of travertine.

95

BELOW: *Library, Bennington College, Bennington, Vermont, 1959.* Pietro Belluschi and Carl Koch and Associates solved the problem of relating a contemporary structure to a campus of imitation Georgian buildings by keeping to the scale of the other buildings and using similar textures and color (painted white wood siding). A notable feature of the interior is its soundproof reading booths.

96

Richards Medical Research Building, University of Pennsylvania,
Philadelphia, Pennsylvania, 1958–1960. Louis I. Kahn was
responsible for the design of this highly original structure, a
series of glass and brick towers reminiscent of a medieval
walled city. Exit stair towers at left and right flank a labora-
tory tower and four air-intake stacks.

David S. Ingalls Hockey Rink, Yale University, New Haven, Connecticut, 1959. Eero Saarinen, a creative giant of the twentieth century, was equally great at solving both engineering and aesthetic problems. In the use of reinforced concrete for both these buildings, space cluttering interior supports were avoided.

Dulles International Airport, Chantilly, Virginia, 1963. An innovation in the design of this airport serving Washington, D.C., was Saarinen's invention of movable lounges, which transport passengers from the terminal building to their plane. One of these lounges is at the far right.

99

Munson–Williams–Proctor Institute, Utica, New York, 1957–1960. The buildings of Philip Johnson who designed this museum and art center are characterized by the severity and impersonal quality of the International Style. Although the exterior (ABOVE) gives it a mausoleum-like appearance, it is a logical solution for a museum which needs wall surfaces unbroken by windows.

BELOW: *The spacious central courtyard of the Museum,* lighted through a translucent plastic ceiling.

Chapel, U.S. Air Force Academy, Colorado Springs, Colorado, 1962. The architectural firm of Skidmore, Owings and Merrill erected this striking interdenominational chapel of glass. Its 17 triangular spires both contrast with the low, horizontally conceived Academy buildings, and reflect the peaks of the Rocky Mountains which tower above it.

Kips Bay Plaza, New York City. The two slab-like apartment buildings, with shopping center (at left) and gardens are the work of Chinese-born I. M. Pei. Pei is also well-known for the Mile High Center in Denver, his plans for urban redevelopment in Chicago, and his choice by the Kennedy family to design the proposed John F. Kennedy Memorial Library at Harvard University.

103

Art and Architecture Building, Yale University, New Haven, Connecticut, 1963. The work of one of the country's most creative young architects, Paul Rudolph, this is an imaginatively conceived building housing studios and classrooms. Of poured concrete, its interior spaces seem to flow into one another.

ABOVE: *Climatron, Missouri Botanical Garden, St. Louis, Missouri, 1960.* The designer, architect-engineer R. Buckminster Fuller, calls this a geodesic dome. A layer of transparent Plexiglass is suspended just below the underside of a framework of aluminum tubing. Mathematical principles used by Fuller in evolving his domes result in structures that are strong, light in weight, easy and quick to assemble. With no limitation as to size, they may well be one of the most important building solutions of the future.

BELOW: *Capitol for the state of Hawaii, Honolulu, Hawaii.* A model of the newest state capitol, designed by John Carl Warnecke and Associates in association with Belt, Lemmon and Lo. This dignified and spacious building of textured concrete rises from the water of a reflecting pool. The legislative chambers are on opposite sides of a great central court which is topped by a domed skylight.

13 Americana: A Miscellany

SOME STRUCTURES that are part of the American scene fall outside the mainstream of the development of architecture in the United States. They provide striking comparisons; in some cases regional and in others historical.

A common sight in almost every part of the United States is the barn with its accompanying silo. Barn shapes and the materials with which they are built differ in various regions of the country. This group of farm buildings is near Bird-in-Hand, Pennsylvania.

107

Treeless and sun-baked, this scene in Leadville, Colorado, is
typical of many a Western mining town. Partly deserted
now, with its streets still unpaved, Leadville was a bustling
city during the silver mining boom of the 1870's.

109

In contrast to the bare openness of the Western town at the left is this New England village, with its white houses and church, nestled among wooded hills. This scene is near Lake Sunapee, New Hampshire.

The covered bridge, once a common sight in rural areas, is gradually disappearing from the American scene. Roofs and siding on such structures served to protect their timbers from the ravages of rain and snow.

A twentieth-century suspension bridge, the Golden Gate bridge over the entrance to San Francisco Bay, shows that great beauty and grace can result from the unadorned solution to an engineering problem. The largest, single-span suspension bridge in the world, it has a central span of 4,200 feet.

111

A nineteenth-century mill on the Merrimac River at Lawrence, Massachusetts. Hundreds of such buildings, usually of brick, could be found on the banks of New England rivers from which they drew their power. The simple unadorned honesty of their construction gave them a handsome quality.

113

Dodge Half-Ton Truck Plant, Detroit, Michigan, 1938. Designed by Albert Kahn, this structure of glass and steel is considered by many to be one of the best examples of modern factory construction.

114

Grain elevators in Superior, Wisconsin. Tall, imposing cylindrical structures such as these can usually be seen from great distances, rising from the plains of the Midwest.

Glossary

ACANTHUS. Large-leafed plant of the Mediterranean region, used abstractly in the decoration of Greek, Roman, and Renaissance capitals.

ADOBE. Sun-dried clay used as a building material.

ARCH. A curving structure made of wedge-shaped stones or bricks, spanning an opening and capable of supporting a wall above it.

BALUSTRADE. A handrail, usually supported by small pillars (balusters).

BAROQUE. The style of the late Renaissance (seventeenth and early eighteenth centuries); usually extremely ornate.

BATTLEMENT. Notched wall at top of medieval buildings originally for purpose of fortification.

BAUHAUS. An art school founded in 1919 in Weimar, Germany, by Walter Gropius. Its principles included an attempt to bridge the gap between pure and applied art, and the striving for direct and functional forms.

BESSEMER. Name of English engineer who was one of the originators of a special process of making steel.

BROKEN PEDIMENT. A pediment in which one or both of the cornices are not continuous.

BUTTRESS. Exterior wall support or brace used chiefly in Gothic cathedrals.

CANTILEVER. A beam projected horizontally, supported by a downward force behind a fulcrum.

CAPITAL. Top part of a column, usually decorated, and larger in diameter than the shaft of the column.

CASEMENT WINDOW. A window hung to a frame by hinges on one of its vertical sides.

CLAPBOARDS. Overlapping boards on the exterior of a house, serving to seal out moisture and wind.

CLASSICAL. Style of the Greek and Roman periods.

COLONNADE. Rows of columns connected at their top by a cornice, and sometimes roofed.

COLUMN. Vertical shaft, cylindrical in form, usually used to support some part of a building.

CORINTHIAN. Latest and most ornate of the three orders of Greek capitals.

ACANTHUS

BALUSTRADE

BATTLEMENT

BROKEN PEDIMENT

BUTTRESS

CORINTHIAN

CORNICE

DENTILS

DORIC

DORMER

FANLIGHT

FLUTING

FLYING BUTTRESS

GABLE

GAMBREL ROOF

HIPPED ROOF

HALF TIMBER

IONIC

KEYSTONE

CORNICE. A horizontal projection at the top of a wall; often a decorative development of the eaves of a roof.

CURTAIN WALL. Outside covering, usually of glass, on a building supported by steel or concrete.

CUPOLA. A small structure above a roof, sometimes covered by a hemisphere or dome.

DENTILS. Small projecting blocks or "teeth" used in classical and Renaissance cornices.

DOME. A convex roof, usually hemispheric in form.

DORIC. Earliest and simplest of the three orders of Greek capitals.

DORMER. A vertical window projecting from the roof of a building.

EAVES. The lower edge of a roof that projects beyond the wall underneath.

ELEVATION. Any of the sides of a building.

ELL. Addition or wing, usually at right angles (like an L) to a house.

FACADE. The front or chief elevation of a building.

FANLIGHT. A fan-shaped transom or window over a door.

FENESTRATION. Arrangement of windows.

FLUTING. Shallow, concave, vertical grooves in the surface of a column.

FLYING BUTTRESS. An open-work support used to resist the outward thrust of the wall of a Gothic church or cathedral.

GABLE. The triangular portion of the end wall of a building, under a ridge roof.

GAMBREL ROOF. A roof with the lower part sloping more steeply than the upper.

GEODESIC. Pertaining to a system of higher mathematics used in dome construction, in which the tetrahedron is the basic geometric form.

GEORGIAN. Style developed during the reigns of Queen Anne and the four Georges, 1702–1830.

GINGERBREAD. Ornate wood decoration used in Gothic revival and Victorian buildings.

GIRDER. A horizontal supporting beam, usually steel.

GOTHIC. Late medieval style (thirteenth and fourteenth centuries) characterized by pointed arches, buttresses, stone tracery, stained glass windows.

HALF TIMBER. Type of construction in which spaces formed by the wooden beams are filled in with stones or wattle and daub, the beams being left exposed.

HIPPED ROOF. A roof of four sloping sides.

INTERNATIONAL STYLE. Style stemming from the Bauhaus; characterized by purity, functionalism, impersonality.

IONIC. Second of the three orders of Greek capitals.

KEYSTONE. Stone used at the center of an arch, locking the other stones in place.

LEAN-TO. A supplementary structure added to a building, usually covered by a roof in a single slope.

Lotus bud capital. Top of an Egyptian column, in the form of a lotus bud. The lotus is a tropical water lily.

LOTUS BUD CAPITAL

Mansard roof. A roof having two slopes on each of its four sides, the lower very steep, and sometimes curved, the upper of low pitch; named after seventeenth century French architect, François Mansard.

MANSARD ROOF

Masonry. Construction using stone or brick, with mortar.

Mullion. A vertical division between windows.

Order. Style of Greek or Roman temple.

Palladian window. Three part window with an arched center section flanked by two smaller side sections; named after the Italian architect, Palladio.

PALLADIAN WINDOW

Pediment. Triangular section, framed by horizontal and sloping cornices, usually found at the two ends of a Greek temple, between the frieze and the roof.

PEDIMENT

Pier. A vertical support of masonry.

Pilaster. Flattened column, usually used as decoration.

Pitch. The angle or steepness of a roof.

Portico. An entrance porch, usually with columns and a roof.

Pueblo. Spanish word for town, used for the multiple dwellings of some of the Southwest Indians.

Quoin. Rectangle of stone or wood used in vertical series to decorate corner of building.

QUOIN

Renaissance. Style of the fifteenth and sixteenth centuries, using classical details.

Romanesque. Architectural style of the tenth, eleventh, and twelfth centuries, characterized by heavy stone-work, round arches, barrel vaulting. In England, called Norman.

Saltbox. House shape resembling a seventeenth century salt box, with gabled roof sloping to the second story in front, and to the first story in back.

Scrollwork. Ornate wood trim.

Shingle. Thin, rectangular piece of wood used in overlapping rows to cover roofs and exterior walls of houses.

Spandrel. Horizontal strips between the windows of a skyscraper.

Spire (or steeple). An elongated octagonal pyramid, or cone, that crowns a tower, chiefly on churches.

Stucco. Plaster finish for exterior walls.

Terra cotta. Clay that has been fired and sometimes glazed. Used ornamentally in tiles on building surfaces.

Tetrahedron. A four-sided pyramid, used as a unit in geodesic domes.

TETRAHEDRON

Transom. A series of panes or lights above a door.

TRANSOM

Travertine. A type of striated marble, usually buff and white colored.

Turret. A small tower projecting above a building.

TURRET

Vault. A roof of masonry constructed on the principle of the arch.

Wattle and daub. Building material; a mixture of mud, stones, and sticks.

Sources of Illustrations

Bibliography

GENERAL REFERENCE

ANDREWS, WAYNE. *Architecture, Ambition and Americans*. New York: Free Press of Glencoe, 1964 (paperback).

———. *Architecture in America*. New York: Atheneum Publishers, 1960.

BURCHARD, JOHN, and BUSH-BROWN, ALBERT. *The Architecture of America*. Boston: Little, Brown and Company, 1961.

CAHILL, HOLGER, and BARR, ALFRED H., JR. (eds.). *Art in America*. New York: Halcyon House, 1939.

CONDIT, CARL W. *The Chicago School of Architecture*. Chicago: University of Chicago Press, 1964.

FITCH, JAMES MARSTON. *American Building*. Boston: Houghton Mifflin, 1947.

———. *Architecture and the Aesthetics of Plenty*. New York: Columbia University Press, 1961.

GIEDION, SIGFRIED. *Space, Time and Architecture: The Growth of a New Tradition*. Cambridge: Harvard University Press, 1947.

GLOAG, JOHN. *Guide to Western Architecture*. New York: Grove Press, 1959 (paperback).

GOWANS, ALAN. *Images of American Living*. Philadelphia: J. B. Lippincott, 1964.

HAMLIN, TALBOT. *Architecture Through the Ages*. New York: G. P. Putnam's Sons, 1940.

KIMBALL, FISKE. *American Architecture*. Indianapolis: Bobbs-Merrill Company, 1928.

LARKIN, OLIVER W. *Art and Life in America*. New York: Rinehart and Company, 1950.

LYNES, RUSSELL. *The Tastemakers*. New York: Harper and Brothers, 1949. Paperback edition by New York: The Universal Library, 1959.

MILLON, HENRY H. (ed.), *Key Monuments of the History of Architecture*. New York: Prentice-Hall, Harry A. Abrams, 1964.

MUMFORD, LEWIS. *Sticks and Stones: A Study of American Architecture and Civilization*. New York: Boni and Liveright, Inc., 1924. Paperback edition by New York: Dover Publications, Inc., 1955.

PEVSNER, NIKOLAUS. *An Outline of European Architecture*. Baltimore: Penguin Books, 1960.

SIEGEL, ARTHUR (ed.). *Chicago's Famous Buildings*. Chicago: The University of Chicago Press, 1965.

SPECIFIC PERIODS

HAMLIN, TALBOT. *Greek Revival Architecture in America*. New York: Oxford University Press, 1944. Paperback edition by New York: Dover Publications, Inc., 1964.

HITCHCOCK, HENRY-RUSSELL, JR., and DREXLER, ARTHUR (eds.). *Built in USA: Post-war Architecture*. New York: The Museum of Modern Art, 1952.

MAASS, JOHN. *The Gingerbread Age, A View of Victorian America*. New York: Bramhall House, 1957.

MOCK, ELIZABETH (ed.). *Built in USA: 1932–1944*. New York: The Museum of Modern Art, 1944.

MORRISON, HUGH. *Early American Architecture*. New York: Oxford University Press, 1952.

INDIVIDUAL ARCHITECTS

BLAKE, PETER. *Marcel Breuer: Architect and Designer*. New York: Architectural Record and The Museum of Modern Art, 1949.

————. *Frank Lloyd Wright: Architecture and Space*. Baltimore: Penguin Books, 1960 (paperback).

BUSH-BROWN, ALBERT. *Louis Sullivan*. New York: George Braziller, Inc., 1960 (paperback).

DREXLER, ARTHUR. *Ludwig Mies van der Rohe*. New York: George Braziller, Inc., 1960.

FITCH, JAMES MARSTON. *Walter Gropius*. New York: George Braziller, Inc., 1960.

HITCHCOCK, HENRY-RUSSELL, JR. *The Architecture of H. H. Richardson and His Times*. New York: The Museum of Modern Art, 1936.

JACOBUS, JOHN M., JR. *Philip Johnson*. New York: George Braziller, Inc., 1962

McCOY, ESTHER. *Richard Neutra*. New York: George Braziller, Inc., 1960 (paperback).

McHALE, JOHN. *R. Buckminster Fuller*. New York: George Braziller, Inc., 1962.

PLACE, CHARLES A. *Charles Bulfinch, Architect and Citizen*. Boston: Houghton Mifflin, 1925.

SCULLY, VINCENT, JR. *Frank Lloyd Wright*. New York: George Braziller, Inc., 1960 (paperback).

————. *Louis I. Kahn*. New York: George Braziller, Inc., 1962.

TEMKO, ALLAN. *Eero Saarinen*. New York: George Braziller, Inc., 1962.

General Index

Rockefeller Center, New York City, 70; United Nations, New York City, 72; Wainwright Building, St. Louis (Mo.), 51; Woolworth Building, New York City, 68

States: Arizona, 60; California, 14, 44, 56, 62, 64, 65, 75, 76, 95; Colorado, 5, 76, 87, 92; Connecticut, 17, 22, 30, 34, 39, 40, 84, 89; Delaware, 7, 9; Hawaii, 90; Illinois, 48, 51, 53, 56, 57, 66, 67, 80, 81; Louisiana, 7, 12, 35; Maine, 37, 43; Massachusetts, *frontis.*, 8, 22, 26, 28, 35, 45, 46, 48, 49, 77, 78, 96; Michigan, 82, 97; Minnesota, 54; Missouri, 51, 90; New Hampshire, 16, 38, 93, 94; New Mexico, 6, 13; New York, 11, 30, 36, 37, 41, 48, 51, 52, 56, 63, 68, 69, 70, 71, 72, 73, 79, 86, 88; Pennsylvania, 7, 10, 19, 31, 32, 33, 56, 61, 68, 83, 91; Rhode Island, 18, 47, 49, 50; South Carolina, 20; South Dakota, 5; Texas, 14; Vermont, 27, 82; Virginia, 19, 20, 21, 23, 24, 25, 85; Wisconsin, 42, 55, 56, 58, 59, 98; Wyoming, 5

Steeples, 19, 28, 34, 36

Stores: Carson, Pirie, Scott, Chicago (Ill.), 53; V. C. Morris, San Francisco (Calif.), 56, 62

Synagogue, Newport (R.I.), 18

Temples: Egyptian, 40; Greek, 31

Tepee, 5

Turrets and towers, 35, 38, 39, 43, 44, 45, 46, 49

Windows: casement, 8; Chicago, 66, 67; dormer, 10, 11, 16, 17, 19, 20, 35; fanlight, 7, 23, 28; Palladian, 17, 19, 27; transom, 16

Index of Architects

Adam, James (1730–1794), 22
Adam, Robert (1728–1792), 22
Adler, Dankmar (1844–1900), 51–52, 55
Austin, Henry (1804–1891), 40, 43
Belluschi, Pietro (1899–   ), 82
Benjamin, Asher (1773–1845), 22, 27
Breuer, Marcel (1902–   ), 79
Bulfinch, Charles (1763–1844), 22, 28
Bunshaft, Gordon (1909–   ), 71
Burnham, Daniel H. (1846–1912), 66–67
Davis, Alexander Jackson (1803–1892), 29–30, 37
Downing, Andrew Jackson (1815–1852), 29–30
Filmore, Lavius (1787–1805), 27
Fuller, Buckminster (1895–   ), 90
Gilbert, Cass (1859–1934), 68
Greene, Charles S. (1868–1957), 65
Greene, Henry M. (1870–1954), 65
Gropius, Walter (1883–   ), 74, 77–79, 99
Harris, Harwell Hamilton (1903–   ), 65
Harrison, Peter (1716–1775), 18
Harrison, Wallace K. (1895–   ), 72
Hoban, James E. (1762–1831), 21
Holabird, William (1854–1923), 66
Hood, Raymond M. (1881–1934), 69
Howe, George (1886–1955), 68
Howells, John Mead (1868–1959), 69
Hunt, Richard Morris (1827–1895), 50
Jefferson, Thomas (1743–1826), 21, 23–25, 29
Jenney, William Le Baron (1832–1907), 66
Johnson, Philip (1906–   ), 86
Kahn, Albert (1869–1942), 97
Kahn, Louis I. (1901–   ), 83

Lafever, Minard (1798–1854), 41
Latrobe, Benjamin H. (1764–1820), 22, 29
Le Corbusier (Jeanneret, Charles Edouard) (1887–1965), 72
Lescaze, William (1896–   ), 68
McIntire, Samuel (1757–1811), 22, 26
McKim, Charles F. (1847–1909), 48–49
Maybeck, Bernard R. (1862–1957), 64
Mead, William R. (1846–1928), 48–49
Mies van der Rohe, Ludwig (1886–   ), 74, 80–81
Mills, Robert (1781–1855), 29
Neutra, Richard J. (1892–   ), 76
Palladio, Andrea (1518–1580), 21, 23, 101
Pei, I. M. (1917–   ), 88
Renwick, James Jr. (1818–1895), 30, 39
Richardson, Henry Hobson (1838–1886), 42, 45–47, 51, 74
Roche, Martin (1853–1927), 66
Root, John W. (1850–1891), 66–67
Rudolph, Paul (1918–   ), 89
Saarinen, Eero (1910–1961), 73, 84–85
Strickland, William (1788–1854), 31, 33
Sullivan, Louis H. (1856–1924), 42, 51–55, 74
Thornton, William (1759–1828), 21
Upjohn, Richard (1802–1878), 30, 36
Walter, Thomas U. (1804–1887), 32
Warnecke, John Carl (1919–   ), 90
White, Stanford (1853–1906), 48–49
Wright, Frank Lloyd (1869–1959), 42, 55–63, 65, 74
Wurster, William W. (1895–   ), 75
Yamasaki, Minoru (1912–   ), 82